Emotional Sobriety

What Is It and How Do I Get Me Some?

Steven C

Introduction

For the most part, when those of us in 12-Step[1] recovery talk about "sobriety," we're talking about abstaining from a behavior or series of behaviors that we once engaged in compulsively and destructively. For those of us in substance abuse recovery, if we don't pick up and we don't use, we're sober. For those of us in recovery from "process addictions" (e.g., sex, love, eating, work, spending), sobriety looks like refraining from a spectrum of harmful behaviors which defined our life in active addiction and re-learning how to do some essential life activities (e.g., sex, love, eating, work, spending) in a healthy way. But in all instances, it's a measurable, verifiable framework of commitments and behavior; a person in recovery is either adhering to that set of restrictions or he/she is not. We're either sober or we're not.

My recovery community for the past 20+ years has been Sex & Love Addicts Anonymous (SLAA); in the preamble to our meetings five resources which aid us in recovery are listed, the third of which is:

---

[1] *See* Appendix A: The 12 Steps of Sex and Love Addicts Anonymous (*with minor variations, the 12 Steps are the same for all 12-Step programs*)

3. **Steps**. Our practice of the Twelve Step program of recovery to achieve sexual <u>and emotional sobriety</u>.

(emphasis supplied). I heard that phrase "emotional sobriety" for years before I thought to ask: "What exactly is 'emotional sobriety'"? My examination of that question has led me to some old places (Bill W. got there before me, what a surprise[2]), some new places, and some interesting conclusions.

And, while it would be understandable to think "Well, they're love addicts, of course *they* would need to figure out how to stay sober from their emotions," my research into the topic has brought me to an understanding, first, of the role of emotional sobriety in recovery from addiction (any addiction) and, second, the ways in which emotional sobriety might be considered foundational to long-lasting recovery from all forms of addictive behavior.

This might be a good place to include the observation that emotional sobriety is, for the most part, a "late-stage recovery" concept. In the paradoxical way that characterizes much of the recovery journey, early sobriety from our acting out behaviors both contributes to and challenges emotional equilibrium.

---

[2] "I think that many oldsters who have put our AA 'booze cure' to severe but successful tests still find they often lack emotional sobriety." Bill W., *"The Next Frontier: Emotional Sobriety." (a letter to a friend written in 1956, eventually published in January 1958 as an article in The Grapevine)*]. Reproduced, with permission and in its entirety, at the end of this booklet (Appendix B).

While it's important to get some kind of handle on our emotions even at the outset of our recovery journey, most recovering addicts find that they will only have the bandwidth to seriously address the work of achieving lasting emotional equilibrium after they've established a solid foundation of sobriety from their primary acting-out behavior(s). It's a cart-and-horse kinda thing – until we've achieved a baseline of abstinence from acting out in our addictions, the chances of obtaining sobriety in our emotions remain pretty slim.

In this booklet, I'll examine

- the variety and nature of emotions,

- the role of emotions in the formation and persistence of addictive patterns,

- how "emotional sobriety" has been defined and how that definition might usefully be expanded, and

- how emotional sobriety can be achieved and maintained in recovery.

My hope is that, regardless of the kind of recovery program(s) you're practicing or the nature of the addiction(s) from which you're healing, you will find something useful in the pages that follow.

— STEVEN C., MARCH 2024

Chapter 1
The Variety and Nature of Emotions

A. The emotional spectrum

So, let's start with a working definition of "emotion." I like the one found in Merriam-Webster's online dictionary: "[A] conscious mental reaction… subjectively experienced as strong feeling usually directed toward a specific object and typically accompanied by physiological and behavioral changes in the body." Although I really like the inclusion of the physiological/behavioral aspect of the emotional experience in this definition, I will say that in my experience emotions can either be experienced consciously or unconsciously.[3] I consider the ability to consciously and accurately assess an emotional state to be a key component of "emotional sobriety."

---

[3] Not to pick on the love addicts (among whom I number myself), but in active addiction we consistently label what we are experiencing as "love" when in fact it is an attraction/compulsion born out of fear, sadness, desperation, and/or self-loathing, none of which we may be conscious of in the addictive trance.

As most people know and have experienced, emotions exist on a spectrum – a variety of different states which can be felt at a variety of intensities. While I have seen charts listing as many as 77 (!) groups and sub-groups of emotions, for our purposes here I'm going to stick to the basics: anger, sadness, happiness, fear, and shame.

B. The transient nature of emotions

Volumes and volumes have been written on the origin, nature, and complexities of emotions. What follows is a very simplified overview, based on my own experience, some research, and what I've observed of the experience of others. Hopefully it will serve as a useful foundation for exploring the concept of emotional sobriety. These are the basic elements of the experience of emotions that are relevant to examining the intersection of emotions and sobriety:

1. **All emotions originate in thought.** Whether we are actively aware of it or not, every emotion that we experience begins as an observation (external stimulus) and/or speculation (internal stimulus) that triggers a chain of mental activity that produces an emotional response. Sometimes the emotion "comes upon us" so quickly that we may not be aware of the thought that preceded it, but it is always there.

2. **Emotions produce physiological reactions that alter our body chemistry.** The experience of a particular emotion is accompanied by physiological changes in our bodies.

Happiness results in the increased production of dopamine and serotonin, neurotransmitters that increase our sense of well-being; happiness also lowers our cortisol levels, leading to an experience of decreased stress.

Sadness comes in a couple of forms. "Crying-related" sadness is associated with an elevated heart rate; also with the release of oxytocin and endorphins in the body which act as a counterbalance by producing a sense of physical and emotional well-being. "Noncrying" sadness is associated with a reduced heart rate and increased respiration.

Anger triggers a flood of chemicals released in the body – catecholamines such as adrenaline/epinephrine and noradrenaline – resulting in increased energy, strength, and alertness. Fear similarly stimulates the injection of increased amounts of cortisol and the catecholamines into the system, which creates elevated heart and respiration rates, dilates the pupils, and restricts the field of vision.

Shame triggers a cortisol response, enhancing the brain's use of glucose (sugar) and slowing functions that would be nonessential or harmful in a fight-or-flight situation.

It is very useful to understand that our emotions can be complex, multi-layered experiences. These include alterations in our physiology directly related to the biochemical consequences of our emotional state which generate changes in what we say and what we do.

3. **The healthy emotional experience is transitory in nature**. No emotional state is meant to last indefinitely. It is not too hard to imagine the unhealthy effects of living perpetually in a state of fear, sadness, shame or anger (sadly, we may have real-life examples of this in our own lives, in our families or in our networks of friends). As pleasant as it might be to contemplate an eternal state of happiness, life does not appear to be set up in a way that supports that possibility – sooner or later, something is going to come along that provokes an emotional state that takes us out of happiness.

We can also understand this from the physiological/biochemical perspective. As noted above, emotional responses result in elevated levels of various chemicals and hormones in our bodies, amounts of these substances which exceed what constitutes stasis in a healthy body. It is not too great a stretch to imagine that subjecting our bodies to levels of chemicals higher than what our bodies normally function with for a prolonged period of time is not healthy.

From an evolutionary and a mental health standpoint, it is clear that the experience of any emotion is meant to be transient, lasting for a period of time and then fading, to be replaced by the next emotional experience.

C. The foundation of "emotional health"

Before we dive into an exploration of the unhealthy ways in which we experienced and dealt with our emotions prior to and during active addiction, let's lay a foundational understanding of how we might experience our emotions in a healthy fashion – essential groundwork for achieving emotional sobriety.

1. **Emotions are just… emotions.** It is useful to think of emotions as a sensation in your body telling you something about your internal or external environment. While it is customary to think of emotions as "positive" or "negative," I would like to suggest that, in terms of understanding and working toward emotional sobriety, there is actually no such thing as a "positive" or "negative" emotion. Emotions are data – sensations in the body. Emotions have no inherent valuation. Emotions are just emotions.

2. **There is such a thing as an <u>uncomfortable</u> emotion**. Depending on a person's individual background, experiences, and mindset, almost any emotion can create discomfort in a given situation. Most people experience sadness, shame, and fear as uncomfortable in most situations. Some people experience joy or happiness as uncomfortable, depending on the circumstance. It can create unfortunate and unwanted consequences, however, to conclude that "discomfort" equates to "danger" in every circumstance and decide, based on that assumption, to attempt to "fix" or avoid whatever is seen as producing that emotion. Learning how to sit in discomfort is a prerequisite to successful recovery; emotions which generate discomfort are no exception.

3. **There is such a thing as an unhealthy response to an emotional experience**. While there may be no such thing as an unhealthy emotion, we are all subject to having unhealthy responses to emotions. An unhealthy response can be defined as any response to an emotion which does not promote our long-term well-being. Examples of unhealthy responses include drinking or binge-eating to medicate sadness or fear, resorting to violence or threats of violence upon experiencing anger, or losing ourselves in fantasy or obsession upon experiencing the joy that romantic or sexual attraction can produce.

4. **There is such a thing as the healthy experience of emotions**. I would like to offer the following steps as a pathway to experiencing emotional states in a way that supports our long-term well-being and promotes consistent emotional sobriety:

   a. **Identifying the emotion**. What am I feeling? Where in my body am I feeling it?

   b. **Not repressing, denying, or judging** the emotion. Short-circuiting any habitual or "instinctual" pattern of avoiding the emotion in the moment.

   c. **Allowing** the emotion to move through us. As discussed above, emotions are intended to be transient; permitting the emotion to transit through our minds and bodies facilitates a quicker return to equilibrium. This is fundamental to emotional sobriety. (More on this later.)

Chapter 2

The role of emotions in the formation and persistence of addictive patterns

W hat can we say about the relationship between how we experience/process our emotions and the onset and perpetuation of our addictive patterns?

There are probably about as many theories on the cause of addiction as there are addicts: nature v. nurture, genetics v. environment, psychology v. physiology, conscious choice v. irresistible pre-existing condition, the "disease model"… the competing hypotheses go on and on.

Regardless of which theory a person subscribes to, one factual thread that runs through the origin stories of addicts is a foundational experience or chain of experiences involving emotional trauma, cacophony, or dissonance that at some point becomes so overwhelming, so extreme, so painful that finding a way to escape it seems as obvious as diving out of the path of a speeding car. The breeding ground for addiction abounds with factors of emotional dysfunction and maladaptive responses arising out of the environments of physical, sexual, mental and/or emotional abuse that are the milepost markers of so many addictive journeys.

Nor do those environments even necessarily have to be characterized by what typically might be considered extreme circumstances. Personally, I was raised in a white, American, middle-class household. I was not abused physically or sexually, nor would I consider my parents to be emotionally abusive – they were simply incapable of offering either the unconditional love that is a prerequisite to emotional health in children or a framework within which emotions (especially "negative" ones) could be experienced and understood in a healthy fashion. The result was a legacy of sadness, shame, and anger that I was completely unequipped to process in a non-toxic, productive way. I didn't know what was wrong or why, I just knew I felt scared, inadequate, and unlovable and I wanted it to go away. A maladaptive emotional template – including emotional illiteracy and emotional avoidance – can arise from a multitude of different environments.

In both addicts and their families of origin, the inability to experience and cope with even routine emotional states (much less the sadly more common experience of extreme emotionality so many of us are subjected to) is a shared phenomenon. I don't think the U.S. is unique in being a culture of emotional illiterates (even among the "normie" population). I suspect that many addicts emerged from families of origin which, even if not outright abusive, failed to teach them how to process even non-remarkable, everyday emotions in a functional fashion. Add to that the percentage of our brothers and sisters raised in highly dysfunctional and overtly harmful environments and I think you've accounted for pretty much the entire addict population. What we all have in common are two things: (1) an inability to consistently produce a healthy emotional response to our environment and (2) a self-destructive solution to that dilemma which eventually morphed from welcome relief to uncontrollable nightmare.

The response of the vast majority of the addicted population to this baffling, continuous, and unwelcome onslaught of emotions can be roughly divided into three categories:

A. Medicating / numbing them

Human beings are, at a basic level, pain-avoiding/ pleasure-seeking machines. We addicts take this tendency to unhealthy and eventually self-destructive levels. Faced with emotional experiences that we do not know how to process or live with, we devise strategies to avoid or ignore them, or to anaesthetize ourselves to the sensations and the thoughts.

For those of us whose addictions take the form of substance abuse, the "solution" is obvious: the regular ingestion of mind-altering/mood-altering chemicals in the form of alcohol, marijuana, cocaine, heroin, meth, prescription medications, or other drugs of choice. If we don't like the way we're feeling, we drink or drug until we don't feel that way anymore, and then continue to drink and drug to ensure that the unwelcome feelings do not return.

Nor is the ingestion of substances limited to those which are designed solely to alter our brain chemistry. The term "comfort food" was coined to describe the culturally-shared experience of using food to allay feelings of stress, distress, or some other uncomfortable emotion. Those of us suffering from addictions related to food and eating are caught in an endless cycle of eating to escape from or medicate emotions we would rather not face.

Others take refuge in patterns of excessive work, excessive spending, gambling, heedless sexual or romantic pursuit, or any of the myriad other lifestyles we addicts have adopted to not feel how we're feeling.

Regardless of the substance or behavior, the strategy remains the same: to suppress or anesthetize feelings we prefer not to endure. This tactic of ignoring uncomfortable emotions in the hope that they will go away conveys, at best, short-term benefits. As we all eventually discover, those uncomfortable emotions will find their expression, one way or another.

B. Bingeing on them

It is also not uncommon to see addicts who avoid one unwelcome emotional state by indulging/overindulging in another. We can understand this as the act of stimulating production of certain biochemicals through extreme emotional responses with the goal of obliterating the onset of other unwanted thoughts or emotions. This strategy can take several forms:

- **Rageaholics**: the pathology is universal enough to have created a common term in the popular vocabulary. Webster's New Millennium Dictionary of English defines a rageaholic as "a person who gets excited by expressing rage, or a person prone to extreme anger with little or no provocation." While to the uninitiated "normie," this behavior may be dismissed as an "anger management issue" or "inability to control one's temper," those of us with experience in the realm of addiction recognize this pattern clearly: production/absorption of abnormal quantities of mood-altering chemicals (in this case, adrenaline, epinephrine, and noradrenaline) to escape or avoid an unwanted reality.

- **Workaholics/gambling addicts**: what these activities have in common is the person's tendency to compulsively engage in behavior that creates and maintains a high level of stress, sustaining prolonged periods of mood- and mind-altering adrenaline production, often at risk to health and sanity.

- **Sex addicts**: "Sexual behavior releases endorphins in the brain that resemble opiates in that they numb pain and produce a feeling of well-being." ("Biochemistry of Sex Addiction," by Tim Lee LCSW, CSAT-S Clinical Director; available online). Persons addicted to sexual release will pursue this experience relentlessly, at the expense of personal health, financial security, and physical safety. The pathology of sexual addiction is a testament to the lengths to which an addict will go to escape and/or avoid unwelcome emotional states. Sexaholics Anonymous (SA), one of several 12-Step programs addressing sexual addiction, basically defines "lust" as a drug.[4]

- **Love addicts**: the neurochemical response to happiness (release of oxytocins, serotonin, and endorphins) has already been noted. Romantic interaction produces its own intoxicating (literally) variety of this experience, and a compulsive pursuit of romantic intrigue and involvement as a means of

---

[4] Step One of SA: "We admitted that we were powerless over lust – that our lives had become unmanageable."

maintaining abnormal levels of these substances is a hallmark of love addiction.

Addicts have discovered that burying oneself in anger, or work, or sex, or romantic pursuits, or gambling, or spending can serve to insulate a person from unwanted emotions. If we fill our lives with rageful reactivity, or ceaseless motion in pursuit of "productivity," sexual pleasure, romantic intrigue, the next "winning hand" or the next "must-have" material object, we can – for a time – keep the hounds of emotional discomfort or torment at bay.

C. Avoiding them
(sexual or romantic anorexia[5])

Sexual or romantic anorexia is a subset of the addictive experience that seeks release/escape through deprivation. In this context of cataloguing the ways in which addicts attempt to evade emotions, anorexia can be seen as a strategy which intends to avoid emotional discomfort by avoiding circumstances identified with emotional discomfort. Although not exactly medicating or numbing from emotions, it is more of an evasive tactic, still employed with the ultimate goal of preventing oneself from experiencing unwanted emotional states.

---

[5] This section is not intended to encompass or address "anorexia nervosa," the spectrum of eating disorders that is classified as a psychological, as well as an addictive, phenomenon.

Chapter 3

How emotional sobriety has been defined and how it might be expanded

As mentioned in the introduction, it should come as no surprise that the co-founder of Alcoholics Anonymous, Bill W., addressed this topic nearly 70 years ago. His thoughts on the subject were written down in 1956 in a letter to another man in recovery, then reprinted as an article in <u>The Grapevine</u> ("The Next Frontier: Emotional Sobriety") in January 1958. The entire article is reprinted (with permission) in Appendix B at the end of the booklet.

To summarize briefly, what Bill W. discovered (decades after he had found the solution to his compulsive drinking) was that his ceaseless pursuit of validation from other people and from external circumstances had instilled in him a seemingly endless sense of frustration and inadequacy that threatened to rob him of the benefits of his "daily reprieve" from alcoholism. He, like many other people with long-term freedom from the irresistible impulse to drink, "lack[ed] emotional sobriety." The cause of this perpetual dis-ease? Bill wrote:

> Suddenly, I realized what the matter was. My basic flaw
> had always been dependence, almost absolute

16

dependence, on people or circumstances to supply me with prestige, security, and the like. Failing to get these things according to my perfectionist dreams and specifications, I had fought for them. And when defeat came, so did my depression.[6]

From my reading, what Bill W. describes so eloquently is classified nowadays as "co-dependence," that crippling emotional-psychological state in which "I'm only OK if you're OK," and "I'm only OK with me if you're OK with me."

This "absolute dependence" on outside forces (either people or circumstances) to supply a person with a sense of affirmation, worth, or love is a surefire formula for instability and emotional insobriety. The unavoidable failure of codependency as a strategy for emotional fulfillment or emotional sobriety stems from one very simple fact: we cannot reliably depend on approval, love, and affirmation from other people, nor depend upon external circumstances to supply a consistent message that we are capable, loved, or loveable. What this strategy begets is – as Bill W. pointed out – an endless series of attempts to manipulate and control "people, places, and things" which is doomed to failure from the outset, resulting in a vicious cycle of fear, sadness, anger, shame, and resentment. This is the polar opposite of emotional sobriety.[7]

---

[6] Copyright © The AA Grapevine, Inc. (January, 1958). Reprinted with permission. Permission to reprint the AA Grapevine, Inc. copyrighted material in this publication does not in any way imply affiliation with or endorsement by either Alcoholics Anonymous or The AA Grapevine, Inc.
[7] Note that Bill W. came to this awareness *twenty-one years* after AA was founded, further proof that emotional sobriety is a "late-stage recovery" concept.

It's my opinion that, with the benefit of another 65+ years of thoughtful examination, "field research," and hard-won experience in the realms of recovery, we can expand upon this formulation that Bill W. provided us and arrive at an understanding of "emotional sobriety" that encompasses not only the very real dangers of codependency, but the entire spectrum of beliefs and behaviors that put our emotional equilibrium at risk.

I see the necessity to expand the definition/ understanding of emotional sobriety arising from the variety of experiences where a person's response, although not driven by codependency, nevertheless threatens to tip the person over into emotional disequilibrium because of other factors. Some examples include road rage and those situations in which professional or personal loss (failure to get a job or promotion, the death of a loved one) triggers a cascade of anger, fear, grief, shame or remorse from which there appears to be no exit. What is wanted is an understanding of emotional sobriety broad enough to encompass all the circumstances in which our ability to reason dispassionately and act or react in our best interests gets overtaken by our emotional state.

To that end, I propose the following "unified field theory," a definition which I hope will be useful when applied to any situation which threatens our emotional sobriety.

> **Emotional sobriety** is the ability to self-regulate our responses to our emotions; a state of being where our ability to identify and observe our emotions and allow them to move through us without hijacking our thoughts or actions can be achieved

regardless of external circumstances or internal thoughts or beliefs.[8]

---

[8] A very useful summation of this concept can be found on the website "Take the 12," where Rick W. states: "Being emotionally sober simply means that I am comfortable being present with all of my feelings without any one of them defining or controlling me." Take the 12 ("Emotional Sobriety," Rick W., May 6, 2022; reprinted with permission, and available at the Take the 12.org website)

Chapter 4

How emotional sobriety can be achieved and maintained in recovery

N ow that we have a working definition of emotional sobriety, let's look at some of the ways available to us to move toward this and to maintain it once we've arrived. I'll divide this final section into two parts: how the 12 Steps can assist us in this process, and what other techniques/resources are available to bring us ever closer to this goal.

The Twelve Steps

As mentioned in the introduction, my main program of recovery is Sex and Love Addicts Anonymous (SLAA) and in the preamble to our meetings we are reminded that one of the tools available for our use is: "Our practice of the Twelve Step program of recovery to achieve sexual and emotional sobriety."

It is my belief that the Twelve Steps are a divinely engineered series of practices which, if undertaken with rigorous honesty, can lead us to physical, emotional, psychological, and spiritual health. But what are some of the ways that the Steps can help us to achieve emotional sobriety?

As I also indicated earlier, emotional sobriety is a feature of late-stage recovery, available only after we (in partnership with our Higher Power) have achieved some mastery over our addictive patterns, made a searching and fearless moral inventory which we have shared with our Higher Power and another human being, thoroughly examined and catalogued our character defects, and reached a place where we are willing to have those defects removed.

With that in mind, let's turn to the latter portions of the Twelve Steps to see how working a program of recovery can lead us to emotional equilibrium.

Steps 8 and 9

Commonly known as the "amends process," these two steps call for the creation of a list of all persons we have harmed, a willingness to make amends to them all, and then the offering of an actual amends (except when to do so would injure those we have harmed or others).[9] How can this process move us toward emotional sobriety?

---

[9] For an in-depth guide to the amends process, feel free to check out my booklet Amends, Apologies and the Myths of Forgiveness: A Guide to the 8th and 9th Steps (available on Amazon).

Think of the multitude of ways in which we harmed others (not to mention ourselves) during our active addiction. We may have been able, in the haze of our addiction and the depths of our denial, to repress the psychological and emotional consequences of behaving in such an unloving manner towards so many people, but the truth of it is this: somewhere deep in our hearts, we always knew that we were marching away from the pointer of our moral compass, and that this behavior came with a cost.

We could evade the consequences of our actions for a period of time, but not forever. We carried the weight of our misdeeds in the form of sadness, fear, guilt, and shame, and that burden seeped out in other circumstances, at other times, in other relationships and decisions. That emotional baggage influenced us in ways of which we were only dimly aware, if at all.

This is the opposite of emotional sobriety, where we seek to be free from the burden of being controlled or defined by our emotions.

The amends process offers us the opportunity to take responsibility for our actions, own the consequences of our behavior, and present our amends to the persons impacted by our regretful choices. Speaking from personal experience, (and further affirmed by witnessing the experience of sponsees and other recovery brothers and sisters), I can attest to the emotional cleansing that is the direct result of thoroughly, rigorously submitting oneself to the discipline of this process.

As long as we are carrying around the accumulated weight of all the emotions generated by the harms we inflicted on others – buried under layers of denial and suppression as we sought to avoid the reality of our situation – emotional sobriety will be an elusive, if not unattainable, goal. Offering amends for our behavior can and will act as a release from that burden, a way to liberate ourselves from the emotional baggage we have carted around for all these years. We cannot enjoy emotional equilibrium in the present until we have chosen to release the emotional weight of our past. The amends process is a critical milestone in coming to peace with our past and a giant step towards emotional sobriety in the here and now.

I will also note here that, while offering amends to those we have harmed will certainly promote the development of emotional sobriety, it also requires a certain degree of emotional sobriety. Facing those we have injured in our active addiction and vulnerably offering our accountability and our amends is subject to being an emotionally harrowing event in some circumstances. It necessitates a degree of emotional sobriety and firmness to navigate with one's self-esteem and serenity intact. Fear not: working a thorough and rigorous program during Steps One through Seven will bring with it its own degree of emotional equilibrium, sufficient to see the remaining (sometimes challenging) steps through with tranquility and resolve.

Step 10

"Continued to take personal inventory, and when we were wrong promptly admitted it." For many of us in recovery, working Step 10 often takes the form of a daily inventory, conducted at the close of our day. During this inventory, we can ask ourselves a series of questions in order to determine where throughout the day we behaved in accordance with the precepts of our program and the will of our Higher Power, and where our behavior indicates a need for some further work (and possibly some apologies/cleanup work).

The 10th Step inventory can take many forms, but one useful format I've seen asks the following questions:

1. Was I resentful?

2. Was I dishonest?

3. Did I promptly admit when I was wrong today?

4. Do I owe an apology?

5. Did I do or say something today out of fear?

6. Have I kept something to myself which should be discussed with another person at once?

7. Did I think today of what I could do for others?

8. Was I kind and loving towards all?

9. Did I reach out to someone in recovery today to see how they were doing?

10. Did I take the time to connect with my higher power through prayer or meditation today?[10]

Many of these questions touch directly on whether my behavior throughout the day was motivated by my emotional state. There is no reason why we cannot utilize this daily inventory to conduct a status check on our emotional sobriety. The following questions could be added to the list above:

11. Am I holding on to any feelings of fear? sadness? shame? guilt? anger? resentment? Am I attempting to unnaturally prolong a state of joy or happiness?

12. What actions can I take to release any emotions I'm holding on to?

Emotional sobriety is much easier to achieve and maintain if we routinely scan our bodies and our hearts to assess our current emotional state and confirm whether we are, consciously or unconsciously, holding on to any emotions instead of letting them move through us. I'm not suggesting that this is always possible – for instance, someone in the midst of a grieving process may not be ready or able to release those feelings in the moment – but to the extent that it is possible, it is useful for the maintenance of emotional sobriety and achievable only if we develop a practice of consciously assessing our emotional condition instead

---

[10] Borrowed, with thanks, from the Sobriety Freedom website (sobrietyfreedom.com). There is also (of course) a free app that you can use as an aid to conducting your daily inventory; available at https://www.12stepapps.org/10th-step.html.

of ignoring it, denying it, or (worse) trying to medicate it. The 10th Step is perfectly suited for this practice.

Step 11

"Sought through prayer and meditation to improve our conscious contact with a Power greater than ourselves, praying only for knowledge of God's will for us and the power to carry that out." (Step 11 from the SLAA Basic Text.)

What a powerful instrument in our recovery tool belt, this invitation to maintain an intentional connection to the Higher Power of our understanding with the twin goals of ascertaining God's will and asking for the strength to manifest that will through our words and our actions. But how can we hitch our desire for emotional sobriety to this mighty engine?

Step 11 is rich in tools for achieving and sustaining emotional sobriety. Let's examine them:

Prayer

Prayer can look many different ways – from the formal, canonical prayers like the Serenity Prayer, the 3rd Step Prayer and the Our Father to the informal, whatever-way-works-for-you prayers that are your own personal versions of a conversation with God.

But all of them feature a common element: the intention to reach out to and connect with our Higher Power, usually with the twin goals of (1) expressing gratitude or offering thanks and (2) making requests (including requests to ascertain our Higher Power's will).

I think the form of request that offers the greatest potential to support us in our quest for emotional sobriety is the request to turn it over. This usually looks something like: "God, this [insert overwhelming, sobriety-challenging event/emotion here] is too much for me to handle alone in this moment. May I turn this over to You and let You handle it?"

This is a perfect tool for the maintenance of emotional sobriety. Feeling threatened by deep-seated, persistent fear? Turn it over. Feeling triggered and on the verge of a shame spiral? Turn it over. Feeling the onset of a rageaholic tantrum? Turn it over. Let your Higher Power handle the disequilibrating emotional state so you can react to your circumstances with serenity and equilibrium.

Meditation

This practice is also addressed briefly in the "Other Strategies" section below, so let us touch lightly on it here. Two of the chief challenges to emotional sobriety are (1) getting stuck in perseverating thoughts which drive us into emotional tailspins and (2) over-identifying with our emotions to the extent that we become confused between how we're feeling and who we are. Meditation offers a technique to recognize that we are neither our thoughts nor our feelings, that both of those phenomena can be observed from the seat of consciousness where we truly reside, and from that place we can attain states of both mental serenity and emotional sobriety. I highly recommend developing a regular practice of meditation as a core element of achieving and maintaining emotional sobriety.

Conscious contact with a loving Higher Power

Of course, everyone working a 12 Step program gets the Higher Power of their understanding. I hope that woven into that understanding is some notion of your Higher Power as an infinite source of unconditional love, an ever-present font of nurture and support. Nothing can help ground and stabilize us as much as touching into the awareness that we are connected to a power greater than ourselves that loves us without reservation, regardless of our current circumstances or mindset.

Speaking from personal experience, nothing in my life was a greater deterrent to my emotional sobriety than my codependence, my belief that I could not be OK unless you were OK. My reliance on others for my own state of well-being was a constant source of emotional disequilibrium – in essence, making other people my Higher Power. The antidote can be found in the conscious contact of the 11th Step, the intentional effort to derive one's sense of well-being from connection with a Power who is genuinely greater than oneself from whom that loving support is always available.

Step 12

"Having had a spiritual awakening as the result of these steps, we tried to carry this message to [other] addicts and to practice these principles in all areas of our lives." (Adapted from Step 12 in the SLAA Basic Text.)[11]

The utility of the 12th Step in maintaining emotional sobriety can be seen in the two forms of action it recommends. The first form is practicing these principles in all areas of our lives. Hopefully, by the time a person reaches the 12th Step, he or she will have experienced the benefits of working the preceding 11 steps in the form of a less chaotic, drama-filled, self-destructive life. A life shaped by the discipline of recovery can, at a minimum, be less of a traveling demolition derby than our lives in addiction; ideally, a sober man or woman working a solid program of recovery will be enjoying the fruits of a more tranquil, grounded, equilibrated existence as well – all the more so as we take the practices outside the rooms of recovery and into our personal and professional relationships and the rest of our lives out in the world.

---

[11] Slightly revised ("other addicts" substituted for "sex and love addicts") to make it generally applicable. AA regulars will also no doubt catch the revision of "practice these principles in all our affairs" to "practice these principles in all areas of our lives," and hopefully understand why those of us recovering from acting out through heedless promiscuity might prefer not to pledge to "practice these principles in all our *affairs*."

Emotional sobriety is much more attainable and sustainable inside of this way of living.

The second form of 12th Step action is carrying this message of hope, healing, and happiness to other addicts. One of the factors in the addictive pattern that fosters and sustains a constant state of emotional disequilibrium is the inherently inward-turned, isolated mindset. This state of mind is a prerequisite for maintaining the cycle of deception and delusion necessitated by a life of active addiction. Driven by the belief that no one could love us if they really knew who we were, we become trapped in a self-constructed cage of isolation, inescapably chained to our feelings of shame, guilt, fear, sadness, and self-loathing. Emotional sobriety is impossible in such an environment.

Among the many benefits of "carrying the message" is the opportunity to get outside of ourselves, to step off the merry-go-round of self-involved perseverating on our emotional state and connect with others suffering from the same disease. This invitation to shift our focus to the often-painful predicament of those around us, to empathize and offer our experience, strength, and hope in the service of others, is a terrific antidote to emotional disequilibrium, to getting stuck in our own emotional spin cycle. At the very least, sharing my story and listening empathetically to the stories of others almost invariably leaves me with a better perspective on my own current situation; it rarely looks as dire as it did before I began listening open-heartedly to the trials and tribulations of someone who wishes they had what I have. Seldom do I walk away from such an encounter without a restored sense of gratitude and balance – emotionally sober because my sense of perspective has been restored.

Other strategies

What other techniques are available to us to achieve or restore our emotional sobriety? What follows is a list of additional strategies, attitudes, and approaches that can facilitate our ability to be present to our emotional states without being driven or controlled by them.

1. Refusing to dwell on the past

Among the unhealthy habits developed by active addicts which end up serving to prolong and deepen the impacts of their disease are:

- Perseverating on past injuries and injustices

- Shame cycles that use the stimulus of a current imagined or actual trigger of shame to generate a cascading series of shame waves that incorporate past incidents of shame to increase the volume and intensity of the current feeling.

- Projection: I'm including this in the "dwelling on the past" section based on my belief that this practice (which I would summarize as "unexamined, unattended-to emotional states/past trauma triggering overblown, inappropriate responses to current stimuli") is grounded in a failure to address and "clean up" similar wounding in the past. This results in an over-reaction to any present-day triggers that resemble the past injury, compounded by the false belief that the over-reaction has an external cause.

What all these behavior patterns have in common is an unwillingness or perceived inability to come to peaceful terms with the unfortunate circumstances of our past. Whether through therapy, spiritual growth, forgiveness (of others and self[12]), or a combination of these and other forms of healing, developing the ability to not dwell on the past is a key ingredient to gaining equilibrium in the face of whatever is encountered in the present.

2. Accepting the present as it is

While "living in the present" is a necessary corollary to "not dwelling on the past," simply living in the present does not guarantee the firmness and tranquility required to maintain emotional sobriety. In addition to living in the present, an emotionally sober person accepts the present as it is, without becoming mired in the fruitless and egoic pursuit of wishing things were other than they were (which only produces fantasy and/or resentment) or trying to manipulate reality to attain some imagined improvement on things as they are. Both of these techniques are productive only of frustration, disappointment, anger, and sadness. The equilibrium required for emotional sobriety can only be found, as The

---

[12] I have heard "forgiveness" memorably described as "giving up all hope of a better past."

Big Book of Alcoholics Anonymous points out[13], in acceptance.

3. Not letting other people's perceptions, reactions, or expectations define our self-esteem or negatively impact our behavior

I cited, in the Introduction to this booklet, the fact that this is a topic which one of the founders of Alcoholics Anonymous, Bill W., came to identify later in his recovery, and about which he wrote very eloquently. Bill's identification of his "almost absolute dependence" on external sources to provide his sense of self-worth culminates with his following this regrettable pattern to its logical conclusion: "And when defeat came, so did my depression."

I would only add to this succinct description of co-dependency: "And when defeat came (as it inevitably will), so did my depression." It is the inevitable certainty of the failure of this maladaptive strategy that spells doom for emotional sobriety – as long as a person is operating from the false belief that his/her self-worth and lovability can only be sourced from other people, places, or things, that person will remain mired in a vicious circle of despair,

---

[13] "And acceptance is the answer to *all* my problems today. When I am disturbed, it is because I find some person, place, thing, or situation – some fact of my life – unacceptable to me, and I can find no serenity until I accept that person, place, thing or situation as being exactly the way it is supposed to be at this moment. Nothing, absolutely nothing, happens in God's world by mistake." Alcoholics Anonymous (4th ed.), p. 417. (emphasis in original)

resentment, sadness, and shame that is the antithesis of emotional sobriety.

It is only in doing the long and difficult work of extricating ourselves from our deeply-ingrained patterns of co-dependency that we create the conditions in which emotional sobriety can take root and grow. It is only when we reclaim our responsibility for our own sense of well-being that we establish the foundation upon which our ability to observe our emotions and not be dominated by them can be built.

4. Therapy · meditation · mindfulness

I lump these together here for one important reason: any serious pursuit in one or more of these directions will yield an increasing ability to "observe" our emotions and, by witnessing them, differentiate ourselves from our emotional state in a way which fosters and deepens emotional sobriety.

In therapy, a person can learn to recognize and stand apart from their patterns of thought and action/reaction in a way that encourages not becoming stuck in a thought pattern, an emotion, or a combination of emotions and thoughts. In meditation and other practices related to mindfulness, a person can learn that he/she is *not* their thoughts or their feelings; that there is an "observer" within each of us which can stand apart from how we're thinking and feeling in a way that allows us to witness our emotional states and decide whether that's really a place where we want to hang out. Being able to reside peacefully in the present moment allows us freedom from emotional states which are often rooted in unresolved wounds from our past or unresolvable fears about the future.

5. Building a healthy, emotionally balanced life (including the elimination / minimization of drama)

There are two aspects to this that I will touch on briefly. The first harkens back to an observation made in the beginning sections of this booklet: emotions are meant to be experienced *transitorily*. Without attempting to quantify how long that period of transience should be for any given emotion (it will vary based on a variety of factors), it still remains true that emotions are intended to pass through us, not take up permanent residence or dominate our every waking moment. While this process is not entirely within conscious control (e.g., most of us cannot will ourselves to stop being sad or frightened), we can still (a) be observant of our emotional state and take note when any single emotion or group of related emotions is overstaying its welcome; and (b) make a conscious choice to counteract any persistent and unwanted emotional state by engaging in actions that we know from experience lead us into counterbalancing emotional states (e.g., reach out to friends/significant others, get outside of ourselves through acts of service, initiate behaviors that we know bring us peace or pleasure or a sense of well-being, offer up prayers/requests for support to our Higher Power).

A second cornerstone to building a healthy, emotionally balanced life is the elimination/minimization of drama. I'm not talking about the occasional, random intersection of turbulent or intense events to which we are all subject and which are truly, for the most part, beyond our control. To borrow from the vernacular, shit happens. I'm talking about the recurrent intrusion of highly-charged, emotionally-intense circumstances that are subject to keeping a person in a high state of anxiety or fear or excitement for a significant part of their waking hours.

From my experience, this persistent state of upheaval has two main causes. One: the person actively generates drama in their life through their attitudes and actions – by their words and deeds, they rile people up, provoke extreme reactions, and sow seeds of discord all around them. Two: the person "invites" drama into their life through their choice of friends and partners and a choice to remain engaged with a social network that is characterized by high and constant drama – they often claim to be "victims" or "innocent bystanders" in the turbulence swirling around them, but in reality they have (consciously or unconsciously) placed themselves at the intersection of people and events guaranteed to continually produce highly-charged situations and high levels of emotionality.

There is neither time nor space in this brief essay to address the causes or cures for this propensity for drama. Suffice it to say, for our purposes here, that it is the opposite of emotional sobriety. Anyone seeking to develop and nurture emotional equilibrium who finds themselves beset by a seemingly endless series of chaotic dramatic circumstances needs to look at both the origins of this pattern and all potential habit-breaking solutions if they have any hope of achieving the benefits of an emotionally balanced life.

6. Seeing the entire emotional spectrum as natural parts of life that offer an opportunity for personal growth: i.e., creating and maintaining a healthy relationship with all our emotions

I would say that the "post-graduate" level of achieving a healthy, balanced emotional life is creating and maintaining a healthy relationship with our emotions; by which I mean all our emotions: nurturing the ability not just to "observe" an emotional state, but be OK with whatever state is observed.

My addiction was born out of a belief system that told me that if I was feeling uncomfortable, if I didn't like how I was feeling, something was wrong and I needed to <u>fix it</u>. When I couldn't alter my circumstances to eliminate the causes of the uncomfortable feelings, I simply began self-medicating to numb myself to the unpleasant sensations generated by the uncomfortable feelings. I would use drugs, alcohol, porn, and ultimately other people (as sexual and/or romantic partners) – whatever was available – to anaesthetize myself to the discomfort.

For me, these feelings were primarily the "negative" emotions – sadness, fear, anger, shame. But I recognize that for some of us that same discomfort can be generated by joy, happiness, or serenity – "positive" emotions that can feel to some of us like they are undeserved, or illusory, or just a setup for the next one of life's "gotcha" moments.

Regardless of which end of the emotional spectrum is generating this "fight or flight" response in us, the reality is that emotional sobriety calls us to redefine our dysfunctional relationship with our emotions. This can start with an awareness that I ended up adopting as a mantra:

> "Just because I'm uncomfortable
> doesn't mean something is wrong."

This simple phrase became my way of short-circuiting my impulse to flee or numb out from every feeling that pushed me out of my comfort zone. Learning how to sit in discomfort is a critical skill for successful recovery (one word: withdrawal), and that discomfort almost always has an emotional component. Developing a healthy relationship with our emotions begins with recognizing that it's OK to feel uncomfortable (Mantra #2: "My feelings will not kill me.") – it's just data.

This awareness of "feelings as data" can lead us to another level in our search for a healthy relationship with our emotions. It is possible to reach a point in our recovery, in the spiritual journey that is our healing process, where we come to see our entire lives as one continuous classroom, called into session to teach us how to be more loving, nurturing, healthy, whole individuals – to claim our birthright as children of a Higher Power entitled to peace, joy, and fulfillment. Emotions are simply one of the natural components of that life of learning and growth, lovingly supplied to us in all their variety and complexity to help us learn how to heal and grow. When we can embrace this vision, we have truly arrived at a relationship with every emotion we experience that can serve us in every aspect of our lives.

I'm going to close out this section with a poem from the great 13th century Sufi mystic, Rumi, that illustrates this point perfectly. It's called <u>The Guest House:</u>

This being human is a guest house.
Every morning a new arrival.

A joy, a depression, a meanness,
some momentary awareness comes
as an unexpected visitor.

Welcome and entertain them all!
Even if they're a crowd of sorrows,
who violently sweep your house
empty of its furniture,
still, treat each guest honorably.
He may be clearing you out
For some new delight.

The dark thought, the shame, the malice,
meet them at the door laughing,
and invite them in.

Be grateful for whoever comes,
because each has been sent
as a guide from beyond.

— JALALUDDIN RUMI

(From The Essential Rumi (New Expanded Edition), translated by Coleman Barks with Reynold Nicholson, A. J. Arberry, John Moynce (Harper One, 2004); reproduced by permission of Coleman Barks and Maypop Books.)

Epilogue

I hope that you walk away from the experience of reading this book with:

- A better understanding of your own emotional landscape

- A clearer picture of the relationship between your emotions and the roots of your addictive past

- A sense of what emotional sobriety might look like, and how it might be related to your continued recovery

- A vision of how you can use the 12 Steps and other tools at your disposal to obtain and maintain your own emotional sobriety.

Let me say by way of conclusion that this is very much a process, one in which it is wise to be satisfied by incremental progress – heartened by our little victories, not discouraged by the unavoidable occasional setback. Emotional sobriety is too valuable a goal to be sacrificed on the altar of perfectionism – "good enough for today" is a perfectly adequate ribbon to tie on the end of any day where we go to bed sober.

Appendix A

The Twelve Steps of S.L.A.A.*

1. We admitted we were powerless over sex and love addiction - that our lives had become unmanageable.

2. Came to believe that a Power greater than ourselves could restore us to sanity.

3. Made a decision to turn our will and our lives over to the care of God as we understood God.

4. Made a searching and fearless moral inventory of ourselves.

5. Admitted to God, to ourselves and to another human being the exact nature of our wrongs.

6. Were entirely ready to have God remove all these defects of character.

7. Humbly asked God to remove our shortcomings.

8. Made a list of all persons we had harmed, and became willing to make amends to them all.

9. Made direct amends to such people wherever possible, except when to do so would injure them or others.

10. Continued to take personal inventory and when we were wrong promptly admitted it.

11. Sought through prayer and meditation to improve our conscious contact with a Power greater than ourselves, praying only for knowledge of God's will for us and the power to carry that out.

12. Having had a spiritual awakening as the result of these steps, we tried to carry this message to sex and love addicts and to practice these principles in all areas of our lives.

Appendix B
Emotional Sobriety

"I think that many oldsters who have put our AA "booze cure" to severe but successful tests still find they often lack emotional sobriety. Perhaps they will be the spearhead for the next major development in AA, the development of much more real maturity and balance (which is to say, humility) in our relations with ourselves, with our fellows, and with God.

Those adolescent urges that so many of us have for top approval, perfect security, and perfect romance, urges quite appropriate to age seventeen, prove to be an impossible way of life when we are at age forty-seven and fifty-seven.

Since AA began, I've taken immense wallops in all these areas because of my failure to grow up emotionally and spiritually. My God, how painful it is to keep demanding the impossible, and how very painful to discover, finally, that all along we have had the cart before the horse. Then comes the final agony of seeing how awfully wrong we have been, but still finding ourselves unable to get off the emotional merry-go-round.

How to translate a right mental conviction into a right emotional result, and so into easy, happy and good living. Well, that's not only the neurotic's problem, it's the problem of life itself for all of us who have got to the point of real willingness to hew to right principles in all of our affairs.

Even then, as we hew away, peace and joy may still elude us. That's the place so many of us AA oldsters have come to. And it's a hell of a spot, literally. How shall our unconscious, from which so many of our fears, compulsions and phony aspirations still stream, be brought into line with what we actually believe, know and want! How to convince our dumb, raging and hidden 'Mr. Hyde' becomes our main task.

I've recently come to believe that this can be achieved. I believe so because I begin to see many benighted ones, folks like you and me, commencing to get results. Last autumn, depression, having no really rational cause at all, almost took me to the cleaners. I began to be scared that I was in for another long chronic spell. Considering the grief I've had with depressions; it wasn't a bright prospect.

I kept asking myself "Why can't the twelve steps work to release depression?" By the hour, I stared at the St. Francis Prayer ... "it's better to comfort than to be comforted". Here was the formula, all right, but why didn't it work?

Suddenly, I realized what the matter was. My basic flaw had always been dependence, almost absolute dependence, on people or circumstances to supply me with prestige, security, and the like. Failing to get these things according to my perfectionist dreams and specifications, I had fought for them. And when defeat came, so did my depression.

There wasn't a chance of making the outgoing love of St. Francis a workable and joyous way of life until these fatal and almost absolute dependencies were cut away.

Because I had over the years undergone a little spiritual development, the absolute quality of these frightful dependencies had never before been so starkly revealed. Reinforced by what grace I could secure in prayer, I found I had to exert every ounce of will and action to cut off these faulty emotional dependencies upon people, upon AA, indeed upon any act of circumstance whatsoever.

Then only could I be free to love as Francis did. Emotional and instinctual satisfactions, I saw, were really the extra dividends of having love, offering love, and expressing love appropriate to each relation of life.

Plainly, I could not avail myself to God's love until I was able to offer it back to Him by loving others as He would have me. And I couldn't possibly do that so long as I was victimized by false dependencies.

For my dependence meant demand, a demand for the possession and control of the people and the conditions surrounding me.

While those words "absolute dependence" may look like a gimmick, they were the ones that helped to trigger my release into my present degree of stability and quietness of mind, qualities which I am now trying to consolidate by offering love to others regardless of the return to me.

This seems to be the primary healing circuit: an outgoing love of God's creation and His people, by means of which we avail ourselves of His love for us. It is most clear that the real current can't flow until our paralyzing dependencies are broken, and broken at depth. Only then can we possibly have a glimmer of what adult love really is.

If we examine every disturbance we have, great or small, we will find at the root of it some unhealthy dependence and its consequent demand. Let us, with God's help, continually surrender these hobbling demands. Then we can be set free to live and love: we may then be able to gain emotional sobriety.

Of course, I haven't offered you a really new idea --- only a gimmick that has started to unhook several of my own hexes' at depth. Nowadays, my brain no longer races compulsively in either elation, grandiosity or depression. I have been given a quiet place in bright sunshine."

— BILL WILSON

From a letter to a friend written in 1956 eventually published in January 1958 as an article in The Grapevine: "The Next Frontier: Emotional Sobriety."

.

Made in the USA
Columbia, SC
03 October 2024